ECHO OF THE GREEN MOUNTAINS

OF THE

Ukrainian Folk Tales

Kiev
Dnipro Publishers
1988

Луна зелених гір
Українські народні казки

Translated from the Ukrainian
by SERHIY VLADOV.
and MARY SKRYPNYK
("The Miracle
of the Stone Mountain")

Illustrated
by NADIYA
PONOMARENKO

CONTENTS

3 THE MIRACLE OF THE STONE
   MOUNTAIN
11 THE DIAMOND FENCE
24 THE GIFTS FROM THE THREE GRAINS
31 THE MUSHROOM-BROTHER
   AND THE BERRY-SISTERS
42 THE WHITE ROSE
49 VASYL NE'ER-DIE
56 THE THREE BISCUITS
61 LUCIFER'S DAUGHTER
70 THE BRAVE LAD THAT BROUGHT
   THE SUN, THE MOON
   AND THE STARS BACK
   TO THE PEOPLE
80 THE REED-GIRL

Printed in the USSR

Л $\dfrac{4803010200-249}{M205(04)-88}$ КУ 9.171.88

ISBN 5-308-00233-9

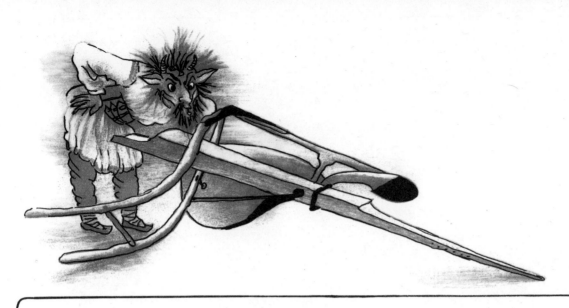

The Miracle Of The Stone Mountain

In this tale I will tell you about a poor man who had three sons: Petro, Dmytro and foolish Fedko. The lads grew up, but all the land that the poor man owned could be jumped over by a rabbit. Poverty so strongly settled into this home, that even a club couldn't drive it out. Nor would sitting and weeping or standing and screaming help.

At last the poor man went to a rich man and said:

"Loan me a pair of oxen and a plough. My sons and I will pay you back in labor whenever you may need us."

"Very well, you will hoe for three days in my fields."

"So be it."

The poor man drove the oxen up to his gate and called to his oldest son:

"Over there, beyond the village, is the broad Stone Mountain. Drive up there, plough it, and seed it with wheat."

Petro drove the oxen up to the mountain. He lifted the plough off the wagon and began to work. No sooner

The Miracle
Of The Stone
Mountain

did he finish ploughing the first furrow, when a dark, hairy hand rose out from the depths of the hill and struck the oxen so hard that the animals, together with the plough, flew head foremost into a deep ravine.

Sadly Petro returned home and told his father what had happened.

The poor man was furious, and shouted:

"Get out of my house! I don't want to see you again as long as I live!"

So Petro threw a jacket over his shoulders and went out into the world.

The poor man then went to another wealthy man. There again he borrowed oxen and a plough.

Arriving home, he called to his second son, saying:

"You are a bright lad. Go to the Stone Mountain, plough it and seed it with wheat."

The second son got into the wagon and drove to the rock. The furrow his brother Petro had ploughed the day before had vanished as if it had never been. Dmytro rolled up his sleeves. He ploughed around the mountain once and began on his second furrow. No sooner did he reach the ravine when a dark, hairy hand rose out of the mountain and struck the oxen such a heavy blow that both they and the plough went over the cliff, leaving but a hum behind them.

Dmytro was frightened. How could he tell his father? The old man would kill him! He threw a bag over his shoulder and ran off to catch up with his brother Petro.

The poor man awaited Dmytro, happy that at last the Stone Mountain would be tilled and planted.

But the day passed and his son did not return. The mother began to weep and he tried to console her.

The Miracle
Of The Stone
Mountain

"Don't cry, wife. Dmytro wants to finish the job and
that is why he's so late."

The next day, foolish Fedko, the third son of the poor
man, suddenly stuck his head out over the oven bed
and said:

"Father, Dmytro didn't plough the Stone Mountain.
The oxen were killed, the plough broken, and Dmytro ran
off to catch up with Petro."

"And who told you that, you fool?"

5

"Nobody. I know everything..."

The poor man went to the mountain to see for himself. Looking over the cliffside he saw the two pairs of oxen and the broken ploughs lying at the bottom of the ravine. He returned home, sat on the bench and grieved for his two sons. All night long he grieved and worried also about how he would be able to pay the rich men back without his sons.

"Don't worry, father," said Fedko from the oven bed, finally. "Tomorrow I will go and plough. Just get me a pair of oxen. I'll sow the wheat, find my brothers and bring back all the animals."

The poor man again went out and borrowed a couple of oxen and a plough. Fedko got into the wagon, and singing, drove off to the Stone Mountain. When he looked down over the cliff his shirt turned clammy on his back. There, at the bottom, lay the four killed oxen and the two broken ploughs. When he had overcome his fear, the lad went to work. He ploughed one furrow and began on his second. Suddenly, out of the mountain, a dark, hairy hand again reached out and prepared to smite the two oxen as it had before.

But Fedko was quick. He dropped the reins and seized the hand. He held it as in a vice, and so strongly that no power on earth could have released it. Then he began to pull. He pulled and pulled till he was out of breath. After much bitter effort he pulled out the devilish creature. Grasping it by the hair, he threw it to the ground and held it down with his knee.

"You scoundrel! How dare you, without so much as by your leave, make mischief for people? Now that I've got you, I'll not let you out of my hands alive!"

The Miracle
Of The Stone
Mountain

6

"Don't take my life, Fedko!" begged the Devil, for it was he.

"My hands have long itched to get a hold of you..."

Fedko drew a pocket-knife from out of his shirt, cut off the tip of the Devil's left ear and pushed it under his belt.

"Now, you Devil, you'll harness yorself to the plough and plough the entire Stone Mountain so that it will grow a crop of golden wheat."

"But I don't like to plough, young fellow. I'll do something else..."

Fedko didn't listen. He took the yoke off the oxen and hanged it around the Devil's neck. Then he cracked his whip at him so hard that the evil spirit jumped.

"Away, you son of the Devil!"

The Devil pulled and pulled at the plough so that his eyes were almost popping, while Fedko marched behind holding the plough-handles and humming a little tune. How long they ploughed, I cannot say, but the cultivated earth on the Stone Mountain became soft as goose feathers.

The sweat poured off the Devil in rivulets.

"Now, Fedko, run and get the wheat, and I'll rest in the meantime," he said to the lad. "But quickly, please."

Fedko rushed home out of breath and standing at the gate shouted:

"Father, quickly give me some wheat to sow, because the Devil has no time!"

The poor man carried out a bag of wheat. He wouldn't give any more because he was afraid Fedko would waste it.

The Devil seeded the ploughed earth, harrowed it down with his tail, then bowed pathetically before Fedko and begged:

"Please, give me back the tip of my left ear!"

"Maybe you'd like a pain in the side too, eh? I want to see my brothers Petro and Dmytro here immediately, or I'll light a candle to your memory!"

"Don't light any candles, Fedko! All will be as you wish."

At that moment an unexpected, terrible gale blew up. The wind ran riot, like that fool at a christening. The Devil sat on its peak and flew off who knows where. But he soon returned with Petro and Dmytro.

"Here are your brothers," he told Fedko. "Now give me back the tip of my left ear!"

"Not so fast, you clumsy idiot, why did you destroy the ploughs? I want them here with the oxen, alive and new!"

The Devil whirled about and sank down into the ravine. In a moment he was back with two new ploughs and living oxen.

"Now, please give me the tip of my left ear!" groaned the Devil. Fedko pulled the bit of skin out from under his belt and threw it to him:

"I don't want to see neither hide nor hair of you here again!" he threatened. "Stick to the ravines and the swamps where you belong, or you'll answer to me again!"

The Devil picked up the tip of his ear and took to his heels.

The brothers got into the wagons and drove home. The poor man was overjoyed at the sight of his sons. Petro and Dmytro sat at the table telling their parents about their adventures, while Fedko climbed up on the oven bed and played with the cat.

The Miracle
Of The Stone
Mountain

9

The next day the poor man went up to the Stone Mountain to see for himself if all was well done. He stood as if rooted, not believing his own eyes, at the sight of the broad field of wheat before him, fully-grown and ripe for harvesting. The stalks were silver and the heads shone gold.

He rushed home and shouted:

"Come on, sons, get your sickles and off to the Stone Moutain! Our harvest is already here!"

Petro and Dmytro set out to work with a will, but Fedko remained behind, sitting on the oven bed.

We don't know what happened after this, because this is where the story ends.

**The Diamond
Fence**

This story happened in ancient times when the landlords still forced serfs to toil in their fields. In fact they
could thrash peasants and torture them, and they were afraid
of neither God nor the Devil. The only thing they were
really scared of was Plague who used to wander throughout the land and reign like a queen wherever she went.
When she came even the greatest landlords would abandon
their palaces and flee in a hell for leather hurry.

Once Plague called on a landlord when he was at home.
But the landlord and his wife managed to save their
lives — they climbed up a tree and waited there while
Plague raged in their house. She chocked all the landlord's children to death. The man and his wife grieved and
wailed, then they buried the children and spent their
lives mourning for them. Days, weeks and then months
went by and a child's voice was never heard in their
house.

Once, coming back home from the fair, the landlord
and his wife saw a child in a ditch.

The Diamond Fence

"Whose boy is this?" the landlord asked the local people.

"His father and mother have been taken by Plague."

"What is he doing in a ditch?"

"Dying from starvation."

"No, he is not going to die," said the landlord. "I shall adopt him."

He took the child into the carriage and headed for home. His wife washed the boy, fed and clothed him in rich garments. He looked so fine that their hearts sang with joy. But a few years later a dreadful thing happened: the boy, for some reason, lost his sight.

The landlord and his wife became heartbroken again. One day the lady said:

"Why should we care so much for a stranger, a blind one at that. Let him sleep in the stable."

The landlord did not actually kick the boy out of his house, but the boy was made to sleep in a corner and fed from an old porringer. He went around dirty and ragged and nobody wanted to speak to him.

Meanwhile, the landlord bought himself a rifle and went hunting to the woods just for the fun of it. Once he found himself in dark thickets, and lo! — a deer suddenly appeared in front of him. The man shot at it and missed. Shot again, but in vain. He shot for the third time but the deer turned to him, obviously unwilling to run away.

This annoyed the landlord greatly. He took aim again but was not able to shoot at all, for a devil snatched his gun, another grabbed the landlord by his arms and a third one seized his feet. The man collapsed onto the grass like a felled tree.

12

The devils did not let him lie there. They dragged him to hell and dumped him in a hole.

A day passed, then another, and on the third day the landlord started calling the devils.

"Gentlemen, will you let me go home, please, for my wife and the blind boy are mourning for me."

The oldest devil answered:

"I'll let you go but first you'll sign a document which states that you belong to us forever. In two weeks' time a great whirlwind will rise near your house, and then you will know that I'm coming."

A devil brought a sheet of paper and an inkpot. The landlord signed the paper without even reading it.

The Diamond Fence

He returned home and for several days he was wandering around his rooms, fields and the garden, happy that all this was his again. But then he became gloomy. His face darkened with all his worries, he would not eat or drink, and he seemed to be quickly aging.

"Why are you so sad?" his wife asked.

"How do you think a man should feel when he has signed an agreement with devils, stating that in two weeks' time he will be theirs. I managed to get away from Plague by climbing the tree but with the devils it won't work. Save me, my darling!"

His wife kept silent. She did not do anything for a long time, just scheming how to save her man from the devils.

Two weeks flew by and the last day came. The landlord did not go to bed, for he knew he wouldn't be able to fall asleep. He sat on a chair, scared out of his wits; even his teeth chattered. All of a sudden something started hooting and wailing and whining and moaning. A stormy wind rose and

13

The Diamond Fence

whirled around the house so fiercely that it nearly tore off the roof.

Somebody knocked on the window and said:

"Come out into the yard, your time has come."

The landlord's wife said to her man:

"Send blind Ivanko, let him go out to see if the wind has torn the roof off the stable."

Her husband understood her at once. He took the boy by the hand and led him to the door:

"Go out, Ivanko, my boy, feel your way to the stable and find out if it is locked."

The man opened the door and pushed the lad right into the biting whirlwind, which picked up the boy as if he was nothing but a straw, lifted him high into the sky and carried him away.

Ivanko had been flying near the clouds for a long time, until, finally, the whirlwind put him down on the ground. Then it turned into a devil who asked the boy:

"Are you the landlord that signed our piece of paper?"

"No, my name is Ivanko. I am a blind boy. The landlord found me in a ditch and took me to his home, but when I lost my sight, his wife wouldn't even let me eat like other people do."

"Follow me," said the devil and led the boy to a well. Then he scooped up a handful of water and splashed it into the boy's eyes.

"Now open your eyes wide, boy!"

Ivanko opened his eyes and smiled.

"My eyes can see! I am not blind anymore?"

"No, you aren't. But you'll have to do some work for us," wheezed the old devil.

The boy felt better.

The Diamond Fence

16

The devil led him to the stable and showed him three horses.

"Every day you'll give the black horse three buckets of embers and three lashes of the whip; the white one should get two buckets of embers and two lashes. The gray horse should only get a bucket of embers, that's all."

The devil gave Ivanko a cat-o'-nine-tails and led him to a spring, all overgrown by weeds. Water was hardly visible in the spring.

"Don't come near this brook and don't try to take water from it."

"Why should I?" said Ivanko indifferently.

They came up to three big cauldrons. The devil hit the biggest one with his stick and said:

"You must spare no wood for this one — it must be boiling all the time. Keep up just a little fire under the other two, but don't you dare try to find out what's boiling in them."

"Don't worry, master, I'll do everything as you say."

The devil left him there. It was so hot in hell that his mouth was parched.

Ivanko was not used to being either roasted or boiled and he just could not bear the thirst. He went to the brook and put his hand in it to scoop up some water to drink. But when he took his hand out he saw that it became golden.

"Some magic!" he thought and lowered his head into the spring. His head also became golden. He pulled his hat down to his ears and went back to the cauldrons.

The gurgling in the biggest one was hardly audible. The boy put more wood into the fire and sat down to relax. But he could not have a real rest, for the anxiety to find out who was being boiled in the cauldrons seemed to be eating him. At last he climbed the stack of wood and looked into the cauldron: there, boiling in pitch were the landlord and his wife. They recognized the boy and started pleading:

"Put down the fire, Ivanko, for our bones are about to fall to pieces."

"Put down the fire, you say? Never!"

"Why punish us so cruelly, Ivanko?"

"You gave me away to the devils."

"How long are we going to be boiled here?"

"Until you come to your end."

Ivanko threw on some more wood and went over to the horses. He found the whip in the stable and began waving and cracking it. Seeing this, the gray horse asked:

"What are you going to whip us for?"

"I don't know. That's what the oldest devil told me to do."

"Don't listen to the devil, Ivanko. Don't whip us, we have a soul just as you have. Sooner or later the devil will turn you into a horse, and then he'll feed you embers and treat you to the whip. We'd do better to run away together. Mount and we'll be off..."

The lad thought for a moment, and agreed.

"First of all untie us from our stalls, for we are honest people."

Ivanko untied the horses and freed the entire stable. He himself mounted the gray horse and tore off at such a rate that hell howled. The herd, released from their captivity, ran after them. They ran like mad across fields, woods, hills and valleys.

The Diamond Fence

17

The Diamond Fence

The oldest devil was sleeping after his dinner. He was awakened by cries which made hell tremble.

"What's happened?" he asked.

"The horses have run away, and the blind lad with them."

The devil leapt out of bed like a scalded cat and tore off in pursuit. His feet hardly seemed to be touching the ground as he rushed after the runaways.

Ivanko began to feel his shoulders burning. He could not stand the pain, and said:

"Horsie, my shoulders are burning. The devil's catching up. What shall we do?"

"Don't be afraid, Ivanko. Try to bear it a little longer... Take out two towels from my right ear. When the devil comes near, throw one towel at his head."

When the devil drew near, Ivanko hurled a towel at him. But this was no ordinary towel: it wrapped itself so tightly around the devil's head that he stumbled on a stone and buried his nose in the ground. He quickly began to unwind the towel. But you can't unwind something when it's twisting like the fastest of snakes. Eventually the devil threw the towel to the ground, but it tangled up his legs as well as any good reins. Once again he fell and smashed his nose. When the devil got himself untangled, Ivanko was already far away. The devil chased after him like a madman. Again the devil was closing in on the fugitives, Ivanko said:

"Horsie, my shoulders are burning. What shall we do?"

"Throw the second towel at him."

When the devil had almost caught up with them, Ivanko hurled the second towel at him. And it did not make life any easier for the devil: suddenly he was so wrapped in darkness that he grovelled like a lunatic in the dirt, the mud and the mire. In the end he looked like a pig in hot weather. He bat his feet on the ground as if he were throwing a fit. Then he ran after them once more, but this time his tongue hung low. He began to burn Ivanko's shoulders with hellfire. The lad shouted:

"Horsie, I'm being scorched so much I'll very likely get burned anyway. What shall we do?"

"Pull the whip out of my left ear."

"I've got it, horsie."

"Throw it under the devil's feet."

He threw it: and didn't the whip spring up, and didn't it sting the devil! He tied himself in knots. The air was filled with the swish of the whip as it did its job on the devil. The latter realized that the whip wasn't going to let him go forward, so he turned back to hell. But the whip chased after him.

The fugitives came to the capital. The horse stopped, caught its breath and said:

"We'll part here, Ivanko. Pluck three hairs from my mane. If you're ever in trouble, just break one of the hairs and I'll come and help you."

The horse flew off while Ivanko, clutching three hairs in his hand, went to look for some work, for he was very hungry. But wherever he went, people turned away from him.

"He's not like anyone else. He is the color of gold."

Once he was walking past the vast royal garden. He spotted the gardener there, bowed low to him and asked:

"Do you have any work for me?"

The Diamond Fence

19

"What can you do?"

"Whatever you say."

"Then trim the flowers and trees. But mind, if you cut anything back so far that it wilts, you'll be a head shorter for it."

Ivanko went around the garden with his shears, pruning the flowers and trees. There were three flowers in the garden which the king's daughter adored. Every morning she would come to gaze upon them. One day Ivanko happened to trim these flowers. Their heads drooped and they began to wither.

The boy was sad. That evening he didn't go to bed, for he was too miserable to sleep a wink. The princess would find out that her flowers had wilted, and the gardener would cut off his head. He went outside and broke one of the hairs. Instantly the horse appeared and asked:

"What do you want, my friend?"

"I'm in trouble, and I want the fence that surrounds the royal garden to be turned overnight into a diamond one."

"Everything will be done as you say. Go to bed now."

The horse flew away and Ivanko soon fell asleep. In the morning he saw that the tall fence around the royal garden was now made of diamonds. When the sun rose the fence sparkled so much that it was impossible to look at it. The gardener paced the ground near it, unable to believe his own eyes.

And then the princess came. When she caught sight of the fence, the girl at once forgot all about her flowers.

"Who built it?" She asked the gardener.

He bowed and answered:

"I don't know. Maybe we should ask my laborer."

The Diamond Fence

20

They summoned the laborer.

"What's your name?" asked the princess.

"Ivanko."

"Was it you who built the diamond fence?"

"Yes, it was."

"How did you manage to do it?"

"I have a force that enables me to build diamond fences."

"Let's take a stroll together," said the princess.

The girl's heart was beating faster than usual. In fact she fell in love with Ivanko at first sight and was not even interested in any diamond fences.

On the following day the king ordered it be announced throughout the world that his only daughter wanted to get married. The man who would bring the finest bouquet ot flowers would become her husband.

From every part of the world they brought wonderful bouquets to the royal palace.

Ivanko became sad, for he had also fallen in love with the young princess. He wandered like a drunk around the garden hoping the princess would come out if only for a brief moment. At last they met and she said:

"If I don't get a bouquet from you I won't have a wedding at all."

Ivanko did not even manage to say a word, for she dashed back to the palace.

When the night fell, Ivanko broke the second hair and the gray horse duly arrived.

"What do you want, laddie?" it asked.

"By tomorrow morning I want to have a bouquet of flowers the likes of which is yet to be seen in the world."

The Diamond Fence

21

The Diamond Fence

"No need to worry, everything will be done as you say. You can go to bed now."

The horse flew away and Ivanko went to bed. In the morning, when he woke up he saw a magnificent bouquet on the table. There were flowers of every hue: white and yellow, and red, and blue. You name the color, and it was there but the flowers also possessed a wonderful quality: they emanated bright light, just like the sun.

Ivanko brougt the bouquet to the palace and put it near the other ones.

The king ordered everybody who had brought their flowers to come to the palace the next day.

Ivanko was blue again: he could not go there clad in his miserable garb.

He broke the third hair. The gray horse flew over to him again.

"What do you want, boy?"

"I'm in trouble again. I want to have clothes the likes of which the richest lords can only dream of."

"Don't worry and go to bed now. You will have everything tomorrow morning".

The horse flew away. Ivanko had a good sleep and in the morning he saw on the bench the garb he had asked for. He put it on carefully and headed for the palace. There were a great many different kings and princes and lords and highest nobility...

Ivanko bowed to the king, to the queen and to the princess. Then he stood by the wall and waited for what would come next.

The king rose from his throne and said:

"Now, dear guests, take your bouquets in your hands and my daughter will choose her fiance."

22

They did as the king had told them.

The flowers brought by the princes, kings and different lords withered right away whilst Ivanko's bouquet was shining as brightly as the sun. He, himself, was so handsome that neither pen nor spoken word could possibly describe him.

The princess approached each contestant, looked at their bouquets but did not say a word. At last she stood near Ivanko and announced:

"I like this bouquet most of all..."

They celebrated the wedding on that very day.

For some reason I just happened to drag myself to the royal capital and heard some lively dance music and singing coming from the palace. Of course, I only went there to drink a glass of peppered vodka, and I was welcomed to the wedding table, had a nice treat and now I have a few stories to tell to the people...

The Gifts From The Three Grains

Once upon a time there lived a wealthy landlord. His fields and forests, cattle and other riches were beyond measure: even the Emperor envied him. The landlord also had working for him a poor laborer named Maxim who lived in a tiny one-windowed hut. Winds would tear the thatch off the roof and the rainwater trickled down the walls. Maxim shared this shanty with his family — which was large — and food was very scarce.

Spring came and it was time to sow but they did not have a single grain in their sack.

Maxim's wife wept and wailed.

"Our neighbors have already sowed and we haven't ploughed yet. You must do something if we are to last through another year."

"Don't worry," said Maxim. "I'll go to the landlord and beg him to lend us some grain. We'll sow that, and then next year we'll reap our own harvest."

"Then what are you waiting for?"

Maxim went to the landlord and said:

"You see, my lord, I have nothing to sow my patch with. If you could lend me just a little corn, please, so that my children won't starve to death."

The landlord stared wide-eyed and shouted:

"Work, and you'll have your own."

"But I work for you day and night."

"Stop that nonsense, lazy bones."

Maxim hung his head and set off for home. There he told his wife about the landlord's answer.

The sun was shining outside, the birds were returning from the south and all around there was merriment. Meanwhile, Maxim and his wife sat by the porch, woebegone, because their children were going around emaciated and as frail as flies.

Suddenly two swallows flew over to Maxim's shanty and started nesting. Maxim caught sight of them and said:

"Poor swallows, why nest under such a ragged roof? The first rain will drown your nestlings."

But the swallows did not understand what was said — or if they did, they kept silent nonetheless. They built a nest, spread some down over the bottom, laid their eggs and hatched out a flock of tiny nestlings. And there was so much frolicking around Maxim's hut!

But one day a dreadful serpent appeared from somewhere and went for the nest. Maxim's children started yelling:

"Daddy, a serpent wants to get our nestlings."

Maxim ran out into the yard, grabbed a mallet and went for the serpent hammer and tongs. He pounded the creature's back until it broke. The serpent only just managed to drag itself back to its dark cleft, and there it bit the dust. The serpent had gobbled down three nestlings but the

The Gifts From
The Three Grains

25

fourth one had managed to escape. Nor was this one unscathed: its leg had been badly injured during the fight.

Maxim took the bird inside, and his children took care of it and fed it. When the swallow was able to fly they set it free to look for its mother and father.

Summer had passed and fall came. The swallows set off to warmer lands. Snow covered the ground. But eventually winter came to an end and the birds returned home to their nests.

Misery had so comfortably settled in Maxim's hut that the family could hardly get by at all.

But one day a swallow hit the window with its wing. Maxim went outside and asked:

"What do you want, my dear bird?"

The swallow dropped a grain on his palm and chirped:

"Plant this in front of your door."

In a minute the bird came back.

It put another grain on Maxim's palm:

"Sow this one by your window."

The swallow fluttered away but soon came back with a third grain.

"Sow this one near the well."

Maxim thanked the bird very much and did everything as he had been told. He planted the three grains and waited for the harvest. On the next day his children got up early and ran out to greet the sun. But immediately they dashed back into the house scared out of their wits.

"Daddy, there's something incredible that's grown there, oh, it's so big, so..."

"What? Are you dreaming or something?"

"No, Daddy, go and see it."

Maxim came out and, lo and behold! There, in front of the threshold, by the window and near the well he saw three enormous pumpkins. He tried to lift them but in vain, for he was no giant.

The pumpkins had already ripened and were shining like the sun.

"Woman! Make the fire!" said Maxim happilly. "And cook us some pumpkin mash for dinner."

Maxim rolled the pumpkin into the hut and sharpened a knife. He cut the pumpkin into two halves and then he could not believe his eyes, for inside was white bread and pies, cheese and meat, sausages and corn beef, boiled and roast victuals, and also sweets and pickles and spices. There was also a bottle of rum. Maxim put all these delicacies on the table but the pumpkin was as full as ever.

After they had feasted to their hearts' content, Maxim's wife covered the magic gourd with a white towel. Meanwhile Maxim rolled the second pumpkin into the hut. He cut it into halves and it turned out to contain garments, the likes of which the richest landlords could only dream of: silk shirts, brand-new shoes, all kinds of skirts and necklaces and corals too. There was everything Maxim and his wife and children could ever wish for.

Maxim's wife was so happy that she burst into tears; then she covered the pumpkin with the finest tablecloth they had.

Maxim rolled the third pumpkin into his shack. He cut it open and, to his amazement, out spilled a heap of gold. He filled a chest with gold, then his wife covered the pumpkin with a cloth.

"Now you children will never starve and I'll never have to bow to the cursed landlord," said Maxim joyfully.

The Gifts From
The Three Grains

He had his wife and children dressed in the best clothes and when he took a stroll in the village he himself was also clad in a rich man's finery, not in beggar's rags. A few days later he started building a new house.

People were mightily surprised by the fact that poor Maxim suddenly turned out to be a man of means and somebody ran and told the landlord about it. The latter came round to Maxim and said:

"Tell me, Maxim, where did you get this wealth from?"

Maxim answered:

"My lord, I never steal and nobody slaves for me. It was a tiny swallow that brought me my riches." And he told the landlord everything that had happened.

The landlord listened to the story and returned to his palace. He craved for greater wealth. So he built a swallow's nest himself and started trying to lure birds into it. Then one day it really worked: two swallows were enticed into this nest; they laid eggs and started sitting. When the nestlings were hatched and had grown a little the landlord became anxious to welcome the serpent. But it did not come. The landlord was getting very annoyed as the birds were about to leave the nest and then how on earth would he catch them.

One day he fetched a ladder and climbed up to the nest. Posing as a serpent, the landlord killed all the nestlings but one, whose leg he only injured. Then he took the wounded bird to his palace and nursed it the whole summer. In the fall he set the swallow free and it soared into the sky.

Fall and winter had passed. Spring came and the birds returned from the warm countries. One swallow flew to the palace's window.

The Gifts From
The Three Grains

29

The landlord ran out into the yard and asked the bird: "What present have you brought me, my swallow?"

The bird gave him three grains and chirped:

"Sow one in front of your door, the second by the window and the third one near the well."

"Thank you, little bird. Now I'll be richer than the Emperor himself."

Three huge gourds appeared soon in the landlord's yard.

He took a hatchet, hit one of the pumpkins and cut it into two halves. All of a sudden a swarm of locusts flew out of the pumpkin; it settled on the landlord's fields and devoured all the plants.

The landlord chopped the second pumpkin. Whoosh! Out burst a flame which first burned down the palace and then reduced the whole estate to ashes.

The third pumpkin remained uncut. People say that it actually is a nest of vipers and that the snakes would crawl out should the landlord fancy coming back to rule in these parts again.

And Maxim lived long and happily ever after.

The Mushroom-Brother And The Berry-Sisters

Once upon a time in a house by a leafy grove there lived a forester and his wife. They had three daughters who looked like three bright berries and they also had a brown-eyed son. Love and harmony reigned in this family. The forester was a cheerful man and his wife seemed to bloom among her little darlings.

Trouble climbs no trees in the forest, no, it stalks the paths to get to people, and eventually it came to the forester's house, too. The man fell ill.

Death had drawn his net round the house in the woods and there was no remedy for it.

The forester summoned his children and said:

"I wont't tramp the grass any more. My time has come. Remember, narmony and health are the biggest wealth. Love your kin and never do any wrong to each other..."

The poor fellow passed away. They burried the forester, and the family's well-being seemed to have been buried together with him. His wife kept shedding bitter tears: how would she and her little children get by?

The children tried to comfort her:

"Don't worry, Mother, we'll pull through somehow. We'll go to the woods to gather berries and mushrooms."

Days passed by filled with grief and tears which eventually sapped the woman's health. She called her children and said:

"When I'm gone, never go far into the forest, for there lives the Wicked Witch, as cruel as a viper. She snatches little girls and holds them captive."

"All right, Mother, we won't go..."

The forester's wife departed. The orphaned children mourned for a long time; then the boy made himself a bow and went hunting whilst the girls were gathering berries. People used to call them the berry-sisters and the mushroom-brother.

Springs and winters flew by; the children had grown up. The berry-sisters had become so pretty that neither spoken word, nor pen, nor the artist's brush could possibly describe them. Their mushroom-brother had become such a handsome and strong lad that when he strolled through the woods and thickets the birds would sing their hearts out.

The Wicked Witch kept watching the berry-sisters day and night, and never let them out of sight. She contrived a way of luring the girls into her trap, and she would have ensnared them had it not been for the Forest Spirit who loved the girls and warned them:

"Never go to the dark thickets. Remember your mother's last wish."

And they would not go but one day they failed to gather enough berries in their grove. The girls were about to head

The Mushroom-
Brother
And The Berry-
Sisters

for home, when the crafty Wicked Witch sprinkled her potion around and suddenly the ground became a red blanket of berries. The sisters also blushed, so overjoyed they were. They kept picking berries saying:

"This is going to last us three days."

"Our mushroom-brother's going to like it."

"We can even sell some and buy ourselves white kerchiefs."

Oblivious of the danger, they had gone deep into the thickets.

The Forest Spirit warned the sisters:

"Come back, girls, come back! dreadful danger is awaiting you."

Alas, the girls were so excited that they could not hear the voice of their guardian.

All of a sudden the Wicked Witch sprang out from under a shrub, seized the eldest sister and the two of them disappeared in the thicket.

"Mercy! Where are you, our darling sister?" the girls wailed.

There was no answer.

The mushroom-brother, who was hunting not far off, heard his sisters' shouts and rushed to help. Calling out his sister's name, he struggled his way through the shrubs looking for the Wicked Witch, but all in vain. Only a young chamois ran out into the glade, cast a woeful glance at them and vanished in the undergrowth. The sisters and brother burst into tears and, grief-stricken, they eventually went home.

Days passed, and then months; the pain had somewhat eased and the girls again started going to the woods to gather mushrooms. The Wicked Witch kept an eye on them,

The Mushroom-
Brother
And The Berry-
Sisters

33

in fact she had never let them out of sight. Once, the girls had been looking for meadow mushrooms for hours but could not find any, for the Wicked Witch had covered the mushrooms with thick grass. The girls were about to start for home when the ground suddenly erupted into mushrooms. The Forest Spirit warned them:

"Keep away from these mushrooms, girls, they'll do you no good."

But the sisters were reluctant to abandon such a good find. They would put one mushroom into a basket, and two others would appear, just begging to be picked.

Having forgotten about the danger they soon found themselves deep in the thickets. Their baskets were already full but the girls went on picking more and more mushrooms.

"We'll gather enough to last the winter," said the older sister.

"If only our eldest sister was with us, she would've been so happy..."

No sooner had the younger girl said these words than the Wicked Witch sprang from under the shrub, grabbed the middle sister and both of them disappeared in the thickets.

From the dark a voice was heard:
"Berry-sister! Mushroom-brother! Save me!"

The youngest sister was crying so piteously that the birds stopped singing and even the leaves did not rustle. Mushroom-brother, who was hunting not far off heard her cry and rushed to help. Alas, it was too late: the Wicked Witch seemed to have vanished into thin air, there was nobody around; only two young chamois came out into the glade, cast their woebegone glances at the berry-sister and the mushroom-brother and then disappeared in the undergrowth.

Mournful, brother and sister returned home.

A year had passed. Once mushroom-brother went hunting far into the forest. The Wicked Witch, trying to ensnare the boy, mixed up all the paths. Meanwhile, his berry-sister had made dinner and was waiting for her brother. But he did not come. She went out into the forest and started calling.

"Mushroom-brother! Where are you?"

The Forest Spirit answered her:

"Your brother will come soon. Come back into the house, daughter. Mind you, the Wicked Witch is after you."

The youngest sister gave no heed to the warning and went on calling. All of a sudden the Wicked Witch leaped from behind the shrubs, grabbed the girl and carried her into the thickets. The poor thing cried and called for help:

"Brother! Save me from the Wicked Witch!"

The mushroom-brother heard her cry and dashed there but it was too late. The Wicked Witch had vanished without a trace.

The Mushroom-Brother And The Berry-Sisters

The boy stood rooted to the spot. He started calling his berry-sister but there was no answer. Only three young chamois ran across the glade looking at him — so dolefully that it pierced his heart.

The mushroom-brother could not feel at home in his own house any more. For some time he gave in to sorrow and grief, and then he went to the forest to look for his sisters.

The Forest Spirit whispered into his ear:

35

"Don't go there, you'll be done for. I had warned the berry-sisters but they paid no heed..."

"I'd gladly do as you say but my heart will not obey. I must go."

The Forest Spirit kept silent for a while and then he said:

"If you really love your sisters so much I'll help you. Listen to me. Head for the crossroads, then plunge into the darkest thicket and force your way through the bushes all day. Go as far as the squat shack that rests on the oak tree stump. There lives an old hag, as ancient as this world. She is my sister Dreamy-Drowsy. She'll welcome you and try to treat you to some delicacies and put you to bed. But don't touch the food or drink, don't sleep a wink, otherwise you will forget everything and become her son forever. Do as I say and you'll find out yourself what to do..."

The mushroom-brother thanked him for his advice and set off.

The whole day the boy forced his way through the bush and in the evening he found himself in front of the shanty.

"Is there anybody living here? I say, let me stay the night."

Out came Dreamy-Drowsy. The boy politely bowed to the old woman and she also greeted him.

The mushroom-brother came into the shack and sat down on the bench to rest.

Dreamy-Drowsy conjured up a dinner:

"Draw nearer to the table, laddie."

"Thanks a lot, granny, I'm not hungry," he said although his mouth was watering.

The Mushroom-
Brother
And The Berry-
Sisters

36

The Mushroom-
Brother
And The Berry-
Sisters

Dreamy-Drowsy made the bed:

"Lie down, lad, and have some rest."

"Thank you very much, I'll just sit here for I am not sleepy at all," said the boy but he actualy felt as if somebody had charmed his eyelids.

Dreamy-Drowsy did her best trying to talk him into going to bed; she sounded as if she was playing cymbals but the boy sat in silence. Seeing this, the old woman said:

"You are a good lad and a good brother to your sisters. I'll tell you how to find them... It will take you three days and three nights to reach the Wicked Witch's house. Don't enter the house but hide yourself in the bushes by the windows. After dinner the Wicked Witch will open the cages which hold the chamois. The three chamois that come out of one cage are your sisters. They will come out onto the grass and the Wicked Witch will go back to the house. Take your bow and shoot arrows at the chamois. If you aim well the chamois will turn into girls again. Take them by the hand and flee. I'll give you a string of dried mushrooms and if you feel hungry eat one — that will be enough for the whole day. Also, take this needle, a pellet and a jar. All this will prove useful to you."

The mushroom-brother thanked her and started out in the direction of the setting sun.

He had wandered for a long time before he eventually found himself near the Wicked Witch's house. The boy hid behind a tree and peeped through the window. The Wicked Witch was cooking dinner. The aroma coming from the house was so appetizing that the lad could hardly control himself, in fact he was about to rush into the house and beg for some food. But then he remembered about the string of dried mushrooms, so he ate one and felt as if he had feasted upon honey.

After dinner the Wicked Witch came out into the yard and started opening the cages. Two chamois came out of the first cage, four out of the second and one out of the third. The boy kept anxiously waiting. Presently, the Wicked Witch opened another cage and out came three chamois. They did not run to the forest, but stood on the grass and glanced sadly at where the mushroom-brother was hiding.

When the Wicked Witch had gone to wash up, the boy raised his bow, took aim and shot an arrow at the nearest chamois. In a flash the animal leapt and turned into the eldest berry-sister. The boy took aim again and shot another arrow at the second chamois. It fell to its knees and turned into the middle sister. Finally, he shot the third arrow and the last chamois lowered her head and turned into the youngest sister.

The mushroom-brother ran up to the girls, who shone like the sun in their beauty, and they could not tear their eyes from each other. The Forest Spirit whispered to them:

"Run away! Hurry! Run as fast as you can!"

The mushrom-brother and the berry-sisters joined hands and fled through the forest.

The Wicked Witch had washed up and went out into the yard. She counted the chamois and, finding three of them missing, nearly exploded with rage. She set off after them and the earth shook with her strides. The fugitives heard her steps and became so scared they could not move. The Forest Spirit whispered to the boy:

"Drop the needle, lad!"

The Mushroom-
Brother
And The Berry-
Sisters

The mushroom-brother dropped the needle and in an instant a dense forest grew up behind them like a thick wall. One could neither ride nor walk through it. But the Wicked Witch had three axes, one made of wood, another of glass and another of iron. She took the wooden one and started chopping the trunks so fiercely that the ax splintered into matchwood. So she fetched the glass one and whacked so hard that the hatchet eventually smashed into slivers. Then she took up the iron ax, but by the time she had made a path, the fugitives were far away. Her tongue was already hanging low but she flew like a storm after them.

"I'll get ya!" she yelled.

And she would have got them but the Forest Spirit said: "Drop the pellet, lad!"

The mushroom-brother dropped the pellet and in a split second a mountain appeared behing them, as tall as the sky.

The Wicked Witch also had three spades: one made of wood, another of glass and another of iron. She fetched the wooden one and started digging through the mountain so fiercely that the spade splintered into matchwood. So she picked up the glass spade and dug until she ran across the toughest of stones and the spade broke into the fragments. The Wicked Witch grabbed the iron spade and eventually managed to make a passage through the mountain.

"I'll get ya!" she yelled and rushed after them like the wind.

The berry-sisters had grown so tired they could hardly move. The Wicked Witch was closing in on them, so the Forest Spirit whispered again:

"Drop the jar, lad!"

The mushroom-brother dropped the jar and, before he could utter a word, masses of water flowed out of it and formed a very wide lake. The Wicked Witch started gulping down the water and eventually drank up the whole lake to the last drop. She swelled and grew as big as a mountain, fell down into the swamp and exploded.

The berry-sisters and their mushroom-brother reached home without any more troubles.

Which brings us to the end of this story.

The White Rose

Once there lived a rich man who had three daughters, and he loved them very much. One day, when the man was about to set off for the fair, the girls gathered around him and asked to bring them presents.

"I want a new necklace," said the eldest sister.

"And I would like a ring," said the middle daughter. The youngest girl kept silent.

"What shall I buy for you, darling?" asked the father.

"Buy me a white rose."

The man left. He sold this and bought that and paid handsomely for the necklace and the ring. But he had not managed to buy the youngest daughter a present, as nobody sold any white roses. He left for home discontented.

The man was sitting on the cart, saddened, when he was approached by an old hag.

"Why are you so gloomy, rich man?"

"Why, one has every reason to be sad when his beloved youngest daughter asks for a white rose, and they don't sell any at the market."

The old hag said:

"Get off the cart and follow me."

Having led him to a gate she vanished. The gate took his whip away from him; then it flung open letting the man inside. He found himself in front of another gate which took his hat from him and opened wide. Having come through the third gate, the man found himself in front of the gorgeous flower bed he had ever seen: there, in full bloom, stood the white roses which he coveted.

The White Rose

"Oh, how beautiful! My little girl will be so happy," said the man to himself, bent down and picked a flower. All of a sudden somebody grabbed him by the arm and would not let go. The man looked back and caught sight of a monster.

"Let go of my hand or you'll pay for it!"

"Don't yell, it won't help," said the monster.

"Why cling to me like a drunkard to a fence?"

"Be reasonable," said the dreadful creature.

"Swear that the girl for whom you've picked the white rose will come here tomorrow. Otherwise I will not let you go, and your daughter will die in three days."

As if one trouble was not enough!

The man had to give in.

"I swear, she will come..."

The monster let him go. The man came home and gave the daughters their present but he was utterly horrified by the thought that he would have to give his beloved daughter to the monster.

"Why are you so sad, Father?" his daughters asked.

"What else can he do but mourn, he who swore that his youngest daughter would go to the monstrous creature that gave him this white rose?"

43

The White Rose

"I'm not afraid, Father. We'll go there tomorrow," said the youngest girl.

In the morning the man took his daughter to the gruesome gate, which immediately flung itself open. The girl approached the second gate whilst her father remained outside.

The flower bed was nowhere to be seen; instead there were stairs leading to a well-furnished room. In the middle there was a table groaning with the most exquisite delicacies.

The girl, although very hungry, did not touch anything. She sat on a chair and started waiting.

Suddenly an ancient bearded man with a crooked nose stepped in. He was so disgusting and repulsive it was unbearable even to look at him. He came up to her and asked:

"Could you fall in love with me?"

The girl turned away and answered:

"No, I could not."

Crestfallen, the old man left. On the next night he dragged himself in again, looking even more miserable.

"Could you fall in love with me?"

"No," said the girl.

A tear trickled down the long beard. The man did not say a word and went out of the room.

On the third night he duly turned up again. He stood at the threshold, anguished, and started begging:

"Pray, love me, young beauty."

She kept silent. The old man was waiting and tears kept running down his long beard.

The girl turned to him and said quietly:

"I could fall in love with you..."

In a flash the old man turned into a white pigeon.

The White Rose

He took wing, then settled on the girl's shoulder. The pigeon could talk the way people do, and he told her how happy he was, and he also thanked the girl profusely for falling in love with him. The pigeon was good fun and he entertained her a great deal.

Once she said to him:

"I want to see my father and sisters. Would you let me visit them?"

The pigeon said:

"I will let you but you must be back by the time the sun is about to set. If you don't come it will be the worse for me. Take this flower; if it whithers you'll know that I'm dead."

"I will come back!" promised the girl.

45

The White Rose

The pigeon also said:

"It may happen that you will find me dead. Don't be frightened and don't mourn. Prick your little finger with a needle and let a tiny drop of your blood drip on my forehead above the right eye."

The girl stroked the pigeon, took the flower and headed for her father's home.

Her sisters were overjoyed to see their sister alive and also very much surprised to discover that her husband was a pigeon. When she had spent some time with her loved ones, the girl started getting things ready for her return. Her sisters would not let her go, begging her to stay longer.

Dark clouds had overcast the sky and completely obscured the sun. The girl did not know the time and was totally unaware that she ought to have set off already. Evening had fallen but she was still on her way. The flower in her hand had withered. The trees kept whispering:

"Why have you deceived the pigeon? He has died pining for you!"

The swallows circled above her head and chirped:

"Why have you deceived the pigeon? He has died pining for you!"

The stream kept murmuring mournfully:

"He's dead..., he's dead..."

The girl dashed into the room. The pigeon did not descend onto her shoulder: he was lying dead on the window sill.

"He'd been looking out for me," she whispered. "He'd been waiting, but not long enough."

She took a needle and pricked her little finger. A drop of blood dripped onto the pigeon's forehead above the right eye. That very moment a very handsome

lad seemed to have grown up from the earth. He stood in front of her, a young Cossack, as strong as a sycamore tree and as joyful as the sun. He embraced her and said:

"You have destroyed the spell cast by an evil enchantress and you have also saved my life. Will you become my wife?"

The girl gave him her hand and said:

"Let's go to my father, I want him to give us his blessing."

So they did, and the girl's father and sisters were as happy as little children. They threw a wedding party the likes of which their fellow-villagers had never seen. The young couple lived in peace and harmony like two love-birds, in fact they never quarreled at all. Maybe they are still living, if they are not dead of course.

**Vasyl
Ne'er-die**

Once there lived a very poor peasant named Vasyl who was called Ne'er-die. His shack swarmed with children; in fact he had ten of them. It was very hard to feed this lot and still harder to clothe them all. Vasyl used to buy them a pair of boots for winter. One child would put them on, run out into the yard to play a little, and then he would run back into the hut to give the boots to the next child in line... Throughout the whole day the boots would work very hard.

Vasyl Ne'er-die always wandered around hungry and shabby.

Once he went to the forest for firewood. He had been uprooting the stumps all day long and became so exhausted he could hardly stand on his feet. Vasyl sat on the oak tree stump to get some rest, then he spat in anguish and said:

"To hell with this life! I wish Death would come for me. I wonder what he is waiting for; perhaps he has forgotten all about me."

Vasyl Ne'er-die

"But I am here, Vasyl." The man heard an ancient and wheezy voice and somebody placed a bony, freezing hand on his shoulder.

The man turned round and saw Death.

Vasyl lost his breath — so scared was he.

"Why call for me?" asked Death.

Vasyl told him about his misery.

"I don't want to live anymore. Why should I?"

"Oh, no! You can't die now, Vasyl. Remember, you have your hut full of little children. Who do you think will feed them? You'd better become my friend and I'll help you to chase off misery."

"Agreed!"

"I'll make a doctor out of you. You'll go from village to village and treat the diseases for a fee, of course."

"What kind of doctor am I going to be? I know as much about medicines as a donkey knows about the Bible."

"You won't have to know much", answered Death. "Just remember that I'm with you. But I'll remain invisible to everybody; only you will see me. If I stand by the head of the sick man you circle three times around the bed and say: 'Well, uncle, you won't get by this time. I'm afraid it's time for you to go.' If I stand by his feet you can cry out happily: 'O-ho, good man! I'll pull you through. You'll live a long life!'"

Vasyl glanced at Death suspiciously.

"I know your kind. You'll keep me company for some time and then abandon me like a torn rag on a fence."

"I swear," said Death raising his brittle splinter-like hand over the ancient oak tree stump.

On the next day Vasyl took a stick and went to see a sick man who already had one foot in the grave.

"I am a doctor," he said to the man's wife and children who were sitting grief-stricken on a bench. "Go out into the yard — I don't want to be disturbed."

So they did. Vasyl cast a glance and saw Death standing by the sick man's head. He took the stick in his hands and fetched a horrible blow on the Grim Reaper's shoulders.

"What do you think you're doing, you wretched thing? Can't you see he has little children? Stand by his feet! Hurry!"

Death quietly sat where he was told to.

Vasyl examined the sick man and said:

"In three days you'll go to the fields to sow."

It came true: three days later the farmer was ploughing and sowing again.

Meanwhile Vasyl went to see other ill people. Death preferred not to stand by the heads of the diseased, being afraid of a new beating. By that time the door in Vasyl's hut would not remain closed for long: people from all parts used to come and beg him for help. He would never be allowed to leave their houses empty-handed: they paid him with a heap of good things, and also thanked him profusely for his help.

Death accompanied the man everywhere looking really woeful, as he was beginning to hate his partner. But he could not do anything: he had taken a vow in front of the oak tree stump. Once he said to Vasyl:

"We've been good friends for a number of years, but you've never invited me to your place."

"Do come on Sunday," answered the man.

"Good, I'll come," said Death excitedly.

On Sunday Death, arrayed in a white outfit, dragged himself to see his friend. He had a really good time, eating

Vasyl Ne'er-die

51

and drinking and singing songs. The man showed him his household and his many children who did not have to grow up in hunger or misery any more. Then Vasyl asked:

"When shall I pay a visit to you?"

"Come next Sunday to the place where we met the first time."

"All right!"

Ne'er-die put on his Sunday best: a new jerkin, a straw hat and brand-new boots and went to see Death. The latter was already waiting for him by the ancient oak tree stump. From there he led the man to his palace. They trudged through the dark forests by the deep gorges, crossed the rotting swamps and jumped over the gulches and bottomless abysses. Finally they found themselves in front of a snow-white castle.

"This is my palace," said Death proudly.

There were a lot of guests inside: kings and princes and ministers. Their pallid faces seemed to be covered with flour, and their eyes were flashing like torches. The guests ate and drank, sang songs and leaped around like goats that are about to be slaughtered.

"Garbage!" said Vasyl. "Nobody to rest eyes on. Will you show me your household?"

Death took him around the palace. Vasyl had seen all the rooms but he was not allowed to enter the last one. This annoyed him greatly.

"Unlock the room," said Vasyl, and at once regretted his leaving the gnarled stick behind.

"Impossible."

"Impossible? You say this to me? What about your vow in front of the oak tree stump? Unlock it like a good friend should or I'll turn this den upside down."

Vasyl Ne'er-die

Vasyl Ne'er-die

What could Death possibly do with such a stubborn fellow? The key rumbled in the lock and they found themselves in an enormous chamber. Vasyl Ne'er-die stood with his mouth agape. Thousands of candles, big and small, flickered there. Some of them were just beginning to shine whilst the others were about to burn out.

"What's that?" inquired Ne'er-die.

"These are the candles of human lives."

"Is my candle also here?"

"Of course it is."

"Which one?"

"That one, which is burning out."

"What will happen when it burns down?"

"You'll die."

Vasyl was in distress. Then he playfully punched Death:

"Come on, be a buddy, give me a new big candle instead of this taper-end."

"Never on earth will I do anything like that!" said Death angrily. "He who was born must die one day. Time and tide tarry for no man."

The man came home pallid and doleful. His wife tried to take care of him as if he was ill. Vasyl kept silent for a long time, then he said:

"The candle of my life is flickering out."

"Can't you replace it by a new one?" asked his wife, and her eyes filled with tears.

"I asked Death but he wouldn't listen."

The woman burst into tears.

"Keep quiet, woman! I'm not afraid of Death. I'll think up something."

Three days and three nights Vasyl Ne'er-die did not sleep a wink nor touch food. He thought and thought and thought. At last he stood up, rolled up his sleeves and started to build something. He made himself a most unusual bed, the one that could be rotated.

When he felt he was falling ill he lay on his strange bed, cast a sidelong glance and saw Death standing by his head. "He's anxious, the cursed nitwit!" thought Vasyl, swirled the bed and Death suddenly discovered he was standing by the sick man's feet. He stood there for some time and went to the other side of the bed. But Vasyl swirled the bed again.

Death started pleading:

"It's your time to go, Vasyl. You simply must die. They will make fun of me."

"No, I'm no fool, I'll only depart when I feel like doing so. So go to hell now, I have other troubles on my mind."

"Some friend! I'll never put my foot in this shack again!" Death left the house, obviously very hurt.

Vasyl Ne'er-die stood up, very much alive and healthy. Perhaps, he still wanders in our parts and helps people.

The Three Biscuits

Once upon a time there lived a husband and wife. They were very poor. The husband would go to work for his master, and once in a while something came his way. Once he said to his wife:

"Tomorrow I'll be chopping wood, my dear wife. Put something in my bag, so I can have lunch and dinner. It's hard work — all day I'll be swinging the ax and the hammer."

His wife baked three biscuits and put them into his knapsack. The man had left for the woods before daybreak, and when morning came he had already worked up a good appetite. He picked up his sack, but lo! — nothing was there.

"My wife must have forgotten to pack the biscuits," he said and got down to work again.

All day he chopped, sawed, gathered up the wood, and stacked it in a pile. And he was so famished you could almost see through him. By evening he was hardly able to drag himself homewards.

Meanwhile, sitting on a tree stump and eating until his ears wiggled was an imp. An old devil came up to him and asked:

"What are you doing here?"

"Eating."

"Eating what?"

"Biscuits."

"Where'd you get them?"

"Stole them."

"From who?"

"From that poor man who was chopping wood here if you like to know."

The old devil flew into rage. He grabbed the imp by the ear and roared:

"I didn't send you to steal from the poor but from the rich!"

"I was on my way to the rich man and it's not my fault that I met the poor one," retorted the imp.

"Not your fault? So you're a liar, too. Go to the poor man and serve him for three years, one for each of the three biscuits."

The imp screwed up his face, cried a while and then stopped because that old devil was such that if he said a word, it was as good as branded on the imp's snout. There was nothing but to obey. He turned into a young lad, arrived at the poor man's, stood at the threshold and bowed.

"What do you want, boy?"

"I'm looking for a job."

The poor man stared at him in disbelief. "And you come to me? The Devil take you! I have nothing to eat myself."

The Three Biscuits

57

"It was the Devil who sent me to you. I'll eat whatever it is you eat."

The lad stood there smiling. The poor man softened a bit.

"But I don't even have anything to clothe myself in."

"I'll go around in what I've got on me."

The poor man threw up his hands. "And just who is it who's pushed such a troublemaker on me?"

"The old Devil..."

"Stop playing tricks on me, boy," said the poor man cheering up. "Go to bed, and tomorrow we'll try to sort it out."

The boy lay on the bench, put his head on his hand and fell asleep.

In the morning the poor man's wife got up being seriously worried over what to cook for breakfast, but then lo and behold! — in the corner stood a sack of wheat flour, a basket of eggs, a big bowl of cottage cheese and an enormous cask of sour cream. The woman nearly clapped her hands — so surprised was she. She awakened her man and said:

"Look what we have..."

The man rubbed his eyes, carefully examined the unexpected gift and said:

"This shack has never seen such riches."

The boy was fast asleep, seemingly oblivious of what was happening around. When the woman had conjured up some pies, the poor man woke up the boy:

"Get up and eat your breakfast, for it's time to leave for work."

After breakfast they took a saw and two axes and went to chop wood.

They worked very fast: the boy would swing his ax and an oak tree would fall down right away. The poor man just stood rooted to the spot with his mouth agape. The woman brought them lunch, and she could not believe they had done so much. By the end of the day the whole landlord's forest hab been chopped down, and stacked. The poor man was paid a pretty penny for it.

Days, and then weeks and months had passed. Then a year, and another one. The poor man, helped by the boy, was doing quite well; in fact he was not poor anymore. He liked his laborer and wouldn't eat a piece of bread without sharing it with the boy.

But when three years had passed, the boy disappeared, vanished into thin air and never came back. This is a good enough reason to finish my story.

Lucifer's Daughter

Once upon a time — well, it was under serfdom actually — in a village there lived a husband and his wife who had a son named Harasym. Day and night, on weekdays and on holidays they sweated away on the landlord's fields withous letting up. In return the landlord gave them a patch of land to sow the little corn they had. Years had passed, and the man fell gravely ill. When he felt that the Grim Reaper was coming for him he summoned his son and said:

"I'm dying, my son. I haven't known much joy in this life, and the only thing you'll inherit is this miserable hut and also a tiny patch of land that will hardly provide you with a plate of thin gruel for dinner. Keep off the landlord's grace and the people's hatred."

Harasym mourned a little, then buried his father, and started slaving for his landlord again. One Sunday he went to have a look at his own tiny plot of land. He walked around, casting a glance over the field, when all of a sudden he heard a pig grunting in the corn.

"Why did you, the cesspit raker, have to come to my field to do your wretched work?" he yelled.

"Grunt, grunt, grunt," answered the pig.

Harasym picked up a stick and banged the pig's back with it.

"I'll lock you in a wet pen and keep you there until your owner repays all the damage."

The pig did not seem to mind at all, in fact it even ran ahead of Harasym, and he could hardly keep pace with it. Eventually, the pig was locked in the sty. A day had passed, then another, but no farmer would come to claim his property. They just don't want to pay for the damage, thought Harasym. Finally, he had grown tired of waiting and decided to let the pig out into the street, so that it wouldn't starve any more, and there would not be any squabbles, either.

Harasym went to the sty, opened the door and there, instead of the pig, was a girl. She was sitting and smiling, so beautiful that the lad stood still with his mouth agape.

"Some farmer," said the girl. "You keep a pig in a pen and would not bother to bring it any swill."

"But I didn't know... The pig... well, it caused some damage... Who are you, anyway?"

"I am Mariyka."

"What are you doing here?"

"Waiting to be set free."

"And where will you go now?"

"To your hut."

"What for?" Harasym was mightily surprised.

"To be your wife."

"Then do come out of the pen."

Lucifer's Daughter

62

The girl came out, gracefully took the lad by the hand and led him to the shack. There she swept the floor, tidied up everything and started making dinner. Harasym just watched her as if bewitched.

In the morning the landlord's footmen came to his house and banged on the door.

"Hey, Harasym, hurry to your master's field!"

Mariyka stood on the threshold and said:

"My man will not slave for your master any more. He has sweated long enough. Now your lord might as well work himself."

The footmen stood flabbergasted, disbelieving the very possibility of such words being uttered. They dashed to the landlord anxious to break the news.

"My lord, Harasym has got married. His wife is as beautiful as a flower but her tongue is sharper than a scythe. She said her husband wouldn't slave for you any more. She also said you would have to sweat yourself."

Lucifer's Daughter

"That's a wise girl! They'll regret it, the rats!" the landlord became really infuriated. "If she is that wise her husband will have to deliver this letter to the Moon and bring me an answer. If he fails to do it I'll set my hounds on them."

The footmen took the letter and went to Harasym. They banged their sticks on the door. Mariyka stood on the threshold:

"What do you want?"

One of the footmen handed her the letter:

"Harasym must deliver this to the Moon and bring back an answer. If he fails to do it the lord will let his dogs tear you to pieces."

Lucifer's Daughter

Harasym felt quite blue, and rightly so: he had never heard of any letters being written to the Moon, to say nothing of delivering them there. Who would know the road leading there anyway?

Mariyka tried to comfort him:

"Don't worry, husband, we'll get by somehow. Get ready to go, then head for the crossroads. At midnight three carriages will pass by. Let the first and the second carriage go past you, then throw the letter on the third one and wait for the answer."

Harasym had followed his wife's instructions. He came to the crossroads and settled on the edge of a deep furrow. At midnight he saw the three carriages approaching him in full drive.

The horses breathed fire, their manes and tails were ablaze and sparks shot from under their hooves and the wheels of the carriages. Harasym waited for the first two carriages to pass, then he threw the letter onto the third one.

When the carts had disappeared in the distance he sat on the edge of a furrow again to wait for the answer. When the third rooster crowed Harasym heard the clatter and in a moment the first and the second carriages shot past him; then somebody threw a letter from the third one. Harasym brought it home, handed it to his wife and went to bed.

In the morning the footmen came for the answer. Mariyka gave them the letter.

The landlord unsealed the envelope and read the golden lines written by the Moon:

Stop tormenting people! Your father brings wood for the hell fire and you are doomed to the boiling pitch.

64

Lucifer's Daughter

The cursed landlord laughed and wrote a letter to hell:

Father, where had you buried your money?

"Give this letter to Harasym and tell him that he must deliver this to hell and bring the reply," said the lord to his footmen.

Again the footmen's sticks banged on Harasym's door. Mariyka came out and asked:

"What do you want now?"

"We have brought Harasym another letter. His errand is to deliver it to hell and to bring back the answer."

Harasym became so downhearted he could hardly stand on his feet.

"But I don't know the road to hell!"

"Don't worry, my dear," smiled Mariyka. "At night you will go to the same crossroads and throw the letter on the same carriage."

Harasym found her words quite consoling as he already knew those carriages. He did everything just the way his wife had told him.

In the morning the footmen came, and Mariyka handed them the reply from hell. It read:

My son, in our garden there is an oak tree and two apple trees. Between them I had buried my gold.

The lord dug out the money and became fabulously rich. He summoned his footmen and said:

"Tomorrow is my wedding day. If this Harasym's wife is as clever as she thinks she is, she will help her husband bring me musicians from hell. I want my guests to dance the way great lords should."

The footmen ran to Harasym's place and banged their sticks on the door. Mariyka came out and inquired:

"Isn't your master satisfied with what my husband has already done for him?"

"No, he isn't. Tomorrow our master is going to get married. He wants to have the music from hell, of all places. If Harasym fails to fetch the musicians his head will roll off."

Harasym was scared out of his wits, and rightly so, for he had never heard of devils playing music. Where would he find them, and how on earth would he talk them into playing?

"Don't rack your brains, darling," Mariyka said soothingly. "At midnight you will get on the third carriage at the same crossroads and it will take you to hell. I'll give you a handkerchief which you will hide on your breast. If you feel scared you'll take it out, wipe your face with it and your fright will disappear."

Lucifer's Daughter

What could the poor fellow do if, on his master's whim, he had to run such precarious errands?

When the night had fallen Harasym duly turned up at the crossroads, sat down on the edge of a furrow and waited. At midnight he heard the clatter of the fiery horses' hooves. Two carriages had screamed past, and, when the third one was passing him, Harasym ran up and jumped onto it. Then he took out Mariyka's handkerchief, wiped his face and felt things were not so gloomy after all.

The carriage whizzed along as fast as lightning. Sparks shot from under the hooves, the manes and tails flaring like burning sheaves.

Soon they arrived in hell. All around there were so many dreadful things going on: souls were being boiled in enormous cauldrons, and also fried, and smoked, and stewed; and the devils stirred them with their pitchforks.

Harasym's face broke into cold sweat, so he wiped it with the handkerchief.

Lucifer's wife saw him wipe his face and asked:

"Where did you get this handkerchief from?"

"My wife, Mariyka, gave it to me."

"It was I who had woven this handkerchief and presented it to my daughter. You are my son-in-law, aren't you?"

"Who knows whose in-law I am?" said Harasym and waved his hand.

He told Lucifer's wife all the details, how he had found Mariyka in the hogpen, fallen in love with her, and also what a pig his landlord was. He told her everything, and then Lucifer's wife asked:

"Why are you here?"

"Our master is going to get married tomorrow and he wants the musicians from hell to play at his wedding party. I have come to speak to them and to arrange everything."

"Don't worry, lad," said Lucifer's woman. "Go back home, take good care of my daughter and be happy."

Harasym bid farewell, got on the carriage and set off for home.

On the next day guests from many distant parts gathered in the landlord's palace, for the lord was going to marry a great minister's daughter. Everybody was ablaze with gold, silver and diamonds. Tables were bending from the weight of food and drink.

All of a sudden twelve shining carriages came into the yard, and each of them carried a musician. All twelve proceeded into the palace, and there they broke into such a jig that the palace seemed to be shaking. All the important guests joined in; even those who had never danc-

Lucifer's Daughter

68

ed and would never fancy dancing had to jig too, as if some evil force was pushing them. The lord and his young wife were nearly hopping and jumping.

The music did not stop for a minute. The grandees had been jigging until their bones scattered. When they had strewn such an area that no raven would ever put them together, the wedding party ended.

And I was there, in fact I was sitting on the roof of Harasym's hut and watched the hullabaloo, so I am entitled to tell this story.

**The Brave Lad
That Brought
The Sun,
The Moon
And The Stars
Back
To The People**

Once upon a time there lived a great landlord with his rich wife. They were enormously rich but as they grew older they became distressed, for they had nobody to leave their lands to. The lady went to a sorceress to ask her for advice.

"There lives a magic fish in the sea," said the sorcerer. "The woman that eats this fish is sure to give birth to a boy."

The lady came home, told her husband everything and then said:

"Buy me this fish."

The lord went to the seashore and asked the fishermen:

"Could you catch me the fish that will enable my wife to give birth to a child?"

"Well, why not? But you will have to provide us with a cask of peppered vodka, if you want your boy to be happy; we would also need a barrel of honey — then he will be loved by girls. You will also have to fill another barrel with money — and then your son will always be a man of means."

"I'll give you everything. When shall I come for the fish? I need it as soon as possible..."

"It's easy enough to talk about getting the fish: catching it is another story. Come in a week."

A week had passed. The lord brought everything the fishermen told him to, and in return they gave him the fish.

The lord's cook was an elderly Hutsul woman. The aroma which filled the kitchen was so delicious that the woman's mouth watered. Unable to resist the temptation and feeling it might be sinful for a cook not to try her own creation, she took a nibble of fish. Then she carried the rest of the fish to the lady.

Months had passed. The cook gave birth to a boy and a few days later the lady also delivered a son.

When the lord's son had grown he went to school, while the Hutsul boy tended geese... He was not even allowed into the rooms where the lord's son played.

Much water had flowed under the bridge, and the Hutsul boy, adored by his mother, had become a strong lad, as handsome as the sun.

One day it happened so that the sun failed to rise in the morning and at night neither the moon nor the stars could be seen in the sky. People went around mournful awaiting Doomsday. Word spread that it was the devils who had snatched the sun, the moon and the stars.

The Emperor dispatched his heralds to all parts to announce the following: "He, who brings back the sun, the moon and the stars, will marry the heiress to the throne."

The Hutsul lad said to his mother:

The Brave Lad
That Brought
The Sun, The Moon
And The Stars
Back To The People

71

"I'll go to the Emperor's court to have a look at his daughter. What if she is not worth getting mixed up with the devils for."

Having arrived in the capital the lad went straight to the Emperor's throne. He stood in front of it and said:

"Your Majesty, I will save the sun, the moon and the stars but first I'd like to have a look at your daughter as I don't want to buy a pig in a poke."

They led the Emperor's daughter in. The lad struck fire from a flint, made a torch out of a splint, looked the girl over and said:

"Well, she's a nice girl, it might happen that... Well, I could jump into hell for her."

At midnight the lad rode on horseback to a great bridge which stood behind a dark forest. He tied the horse to a willow tree, then tore a plank off the bridge and threw it into the water. Then he hid himself behind a bush and waited.

All of a sudden he heard the clatter of hooves. Somebody stood by the bridge and shouted:

"Who wants to destroy my bridge? Come out, you wretched plunderer."

"I will pull down your bridge," answered the lad from behind the bush.

"Well, do you want to fight?"

"Look, devil, you won't scare me with those hooves of yours; you had better give back the sun, the moon and the stars or I'll thrash you within an inch of your life."

"I will not. We'll fight!"

"Why should we spill blood?" the lad went on.

"It would be better if you became fire and I was rain. Let us see who takes over."

"Agreed!" yelled the devil.

Whoosh! A great fire blazed and at once the rain came down in buckets. The fire raged and the rain tried to douse the flames. The rain poured and the fire flared up. The rain came down in torrents and the fire sizzled. It looked just like hell.

But then the fire grew feeble, while it was still raining cats and dogs. At last the fire died down, the heat diminished and the only thing that reminded of the fight was a heap of ash. The lad scooped up the ashes and saw the sun shining underneath. He grabbed the sun, put it under his arm, mounted his horse and galloped off to the Emperor.

Not far from the road the lad caught sight of a hut and decided to find out who lived there. He peeped through the window and lo and behold the room swarmed with witches who were either spinning thread or smelting tin, or practising their witchcraft over a cauldron.

One of the witches was straining her eyes over some cards.

The lad turned into a fly, flew inside and settled on the wall. The witch that was staring at the cards mumbled:

"The cards tell that a young lad has killed my man and snatched the sun. I must make his years shorter! I'll turn into a lonely pear tree in the middle of a field. When he rides past me and eats a pear he will be done for."

The fly flew out of the hut and turned into the Hutsul lad. He hurried to the Emperor's court, had dinner and went to bed. Before that he had ordered:

"Don't wake me up! The sun will do that..."

In the morning the people were woken by the first rays of the hot and smiling sun. People were overjoyed and the birds also started singing.

On the next night the lad mounted his horse and trotted to the bridge.

He tied the horse to the willow tree, tore another plank off the bridge and hurled it into the water. Then he hid himself behind the bush.

Some time had passed; then he heard the clatter of the hooves. Of course it was another devil. He came over to the bridge, cast a glance at the damage and hollered:

"Who stole a plank? Come out thief!"

"That's me!" said the lad stepping forward from behind the bush.

"Looking for trouble, eh?"

"Give back the moon!"

"You'll have to fight for that, you know."

The lad took his time and then said:

"Why spill blood? It would be better if you turned into a stone and I became a pillar. You'll roll down the hill and hit the pillar. If the pillar is crushed you'll be the winner, and if it doesn't you'll give the moon back."

That's what they did. An enormous black stone bowled down the hill and bumped into the pillar so forcefully that the former crumbled up into sand. The lad scooped up the sand and underneath he found the moon which smiled happily at him. The Hutsul did not take it to the Emperor's palace, instead he hurled it up into the sky. There was a lot of rejoicing all around. The nightingale started trilling, the dogs barked and the frogs croaked in their swamp.

The lad mounted his horse and sped to the palace. He stopped by the witches' hut and looked through the window. Inside they were still spinning thread, smelting tin and conjuring, and the oldest hag was telling fortunes with her cards. The Hutsul turned into a flea, leaped into

The Brave Lad
That Brought
The Sun, The Moon
And The Stars
Back To The People

the hut and then onto the witch's head. She kept murmuring:

"This night a scoundrel has done away with another devil. I'm going to get even with him. I'll tell the sun to heat like mad; meanwhile I shall turn into a well in the field. He'll quench his thirst and will explode into four pieces."

The flea leapt out of the hut and turned into the lad again. He mounted his horse and galloped straight to the palace.

On the third night he was on the bridge again. He tore the last plank off the bridge and hurled it into the water.

The lad did not have to wait long for a devil. He trotted up to the bridge and started shouting:

"Who's wrecking my bridge here?"

"I am," said the lad stepping forward from behind the bush.

"What's so special about this particular bridge?"

"I want you to return the stars to the sky."

"Oh, no! You'll have to fight with me first!"

"You must be out of your mind, devil," said the Hutsul. "I've done it twice already. I hope I'll be able to take care of you as well. Perhaps you'll give the stars back in an amicable way."

"We must fight!"

"Well, if you insist then tie me up with the strongest oxen-reins. I'll break them as if they are just gossamer."

The devil tied the lad up with the toughest ropes and also made such intricate knots that a hundred devils would be unable to untie them.

"If you don't break loose I'll throw you into the river," threatened the devil.

"All right! You turn away now..."

The devil stood with his back to the lad. The latter had a small dagger hidden in his fist. In a flash he cut all the ropes, shook them off and said:

"I guess I've done it."

The devil was scared out of his wits. His face turned white and he started shivering as if he had a fever.

"Now you can tie me up," he babbled.

The Hutsul wrapped the devil into ropes the way potter does with the holey pots. Then he turned away and cried:

"Tear!"

The devil made such an effort that his eyes nearly popped out of their sockets. He threw himself onto the ground, rubbed the ropes against stones and howled in rage like a rabid dog, but nothing would help.

"You should've eaten more porridge, then maybe..." The lad teased the devil. "Give the stars back if you don't want to be done for."

"All right, you can take them."

"Where are they?"

"On the horse's back under the saddle."

The lad took the stars out and started counting them. He had been moving them from one heap to another for a long time. Now it's hard to say exactly how many stars there were, but the lad knew for a fact that one was missing.

"Where's the star?" roared the Hutsul at the devil.

"They're all there."

"Lies! One's missing. You had better say where it is now or I'll teach you what's what."

The devil realized that things were taking a bad turn and that the Hutsul was not born yesterday. Finaly he had to tell the truth:

"I presented one to my beloved witch."

The lad did not hesitate: he placed the tied up devil on the horse's back, saddled up himself and sped to the witch's hut. They stopped by the window and listened to the witch babble over the cards:

"Oh darn it! The third devil has vanished. Perhaps the Hutsul has done for him."

"I am here!" yelled the devil.

"Oh, my darling! Come right in!"

"But I can't, my love. I'm tied up. Now give this lad the star that I presented you and beg him to let me go."

The Hutsul went inside and the witch handed him the star.

"Untie my lover," she pleaded.

"I still need him."

The whole night the Hutsul had been hurling the stars up into the sky. He wanted each star to be in its proper place. When he had finished his work the sun was already rising. He shoved the devil into the sack and headed for the capital.

People thanked him for the sun, the moon and the stars. Only the innkeepers, the Emperor's ministers and the thieves did not thank the lad, for it had been easier to cheat in the dark.

The lad untied the devil and said:

"Now, devil, gather all the innkeepers, ministers and thieves together. Then dip them into pitch, roll them in feathers and show them at marketplaces for three days and three nights."

The devil leapt out of the sack and rushed to fulfill the order.

The Hutsul went to the palace. He stood in front of the throne and said:

"Your Majesty, I've done everything. The sun, the moon and the stars are where they belong. Now I must bring my mother. I want her to have a look at your heiress and say if she wants to have her for a daughter-in-law."

"Let it be so," agreed the Emperor.

The Hutsul set off for his home. The sun was red-hot, as if angry with somebody. The lad saw a pear tree bent under ripe fruits but he did not even come up to it. The thirst was unbearable but, having seen the well with water which was as clear as crystal, he just went past it.

He brougt his mother to the Emperor's court. It turned out that she approved of her son's choice.

The world had never seen anything like the brave Hutsul's wedding. And that's natural, of course!

The Reed-Girl

Once in a village there lived an orphan named Ivanko. When his parents had died he inherited an old shanty and a tiny garden patch.

In the village there also lived a rich landlord named Snapmuzzle. People always tried to keep away from him and nobody would want to cross his path in any way. Once the landlord stood in front of Ivanko's hut and shouted:

"Who are you?"

"I'm Ivanko."

"Why should you possess both the house and the garden?"

"This house gives me shelter and I live off the garden. Any fool around here knows that."

The landlord thought a little and said:

"From now on you'll be my coachman, for this garden's going to be mine. I'll put my bee hives here."

"But your fields are so many! Why take a sin upon yourself?"

"I don't care a bit about this sin. If you don't want to be my coachman, get out of the village."

Ivanko fried himself several potato pancakes, put a few apples into his knapsack and set off. On the bank of the Prut River he saw a little crane. He came up to it but the bird did not take wing. He took it into his hands and found out that its wing was broken. The crane said:

"Help me, nice lad. I've been starving here for five days and my wounds hurt."

Ivanko cleansed the wounds, then he tore up his shirt and dressed them. After that he caught a fish in the river and fed the bird. He also wanted to build a shelter for it, but as soon as he came to the rushes he heard:

"Don't break me, good lad, maybe the man I am waiting for will come nonetheless."

"Who are you anyway?"

"The reed-girl."

"Who are you waiting for?"

"For my savior."

"Will you show your face, please?"

The voice answered:

"I have shown myself twice... And what happened? Both of them went away and neither has come back yet. I can show myself only once, this will be the last time."

"Let me be this last time. Believe me, I won't let you down."

"All right, look at the top of the reed."

"All of a sudden Ivanko saw a gorgeous girl in front of him. She was as beautiful as the first spring flower but she was also very sad.

"Why are you so grieved?"

The Reed-Girl

81

The Reed-Girl

"A wicked witch snatched me from my father. She wanted me to marry her son, a giant. I said no and fled. Then I hid myself in these rushes but the witch eventually found me and turned me into a reed. To save me from the spell the ring must be recovered and put on the top of this reed..."

The girl vanished. Ivanko liked her very much and decided to help her. He returned to the crane and said:

"I must be going."

"Where to?" asked the bird.

"I'm going to look for something I can't even mention aloud."

"Good luck to you then!"

Ivanko had crossed many fields and forests.

Once he caught sight of a hut by the road. He entered and saw three cats which were tied to three pillars in the corridor. Ivanko patted each of them and treated them to some fish.

"Meow! Meow! Meow!" mewed the cats happily.

A voice was heard from the room:

"Who's teasing you there?"

"Nobody's teasing us. A nice lad has given us some food."

"Then come inside, my boy!"

Inside Ivanko was unable to discern anything, for it was very dark there. He struck fire from a flint, looked around and saw an age-old hag lying on the stove.

"It's a good thing, son, that you haven't just gone by my hut, for there's nobody to bring me water."

"Water, you said? Just a minute, granny..."

"No, you can't go alone, you'll get lost. Unleash one of the cats and it will light the way with its eyes."

Ivanko went out into the corridor:

"Which of you will help me fetch some water?"

"We'll do it in turns," answered the oldest cat.

They set off, and when they had walked some distance Ivanko inquired:

"Say, mog, how come that you're tethered?"

"I can't tell you, the old hag will banish me from the house. Ask the others."

Ivanko conjured up some thin gruel and fed the old hag and her cats.

On the next day Ivanko went for the water with the second cat.

"Say, tom, why are you all tethered?"

"I can't tell you. I'm afraid of her..."

On the third day Ivanko was accompanied by the third cat. The lad gave some water to the animal and also a piece of fish and patted it.

"Tell me, my friend, why are you tethered?"

"I'm afraid of talking, but I will tell you. The old hag is the chief witch. At night all the evil ones fly over to see her and discuss how to cause people still greater harm. They'll have their sabbath today as well. The old hag will stick some wax into your ears, so that you won't hear anything. But I'll tell you everything."

"Tell me, dear tom, has she ever mentioned the girl that was turned into a reed?"

"Of course, she has. The witch even said that there had been two lads who tried to steal the ring from her. She turned them both into stones. They are lying there, near the shack. When the sun starts to scorch the old witch sits on them to get warm."

"What should I do to bring them back to life?"

The Reed-Girl

83

The Reed-Girl

"You'll have to sprinkle the stones with the water of the lake from which no one has ever drunk."

Ivanko made dinner, fed the old hag and the cats and went to bed. Then the witch said:

"Ivanko, the night might turn out to be quite thunderous. I'll stick some fresh wax into your ears, lest you go deaf."

At midnight, all sorts of witches and vampires and imps turned up to hold a reunion at the hut. There were so many of them that the newcomers had nowhere to sit or stand. Ivanko took the wax out of one ear and heard: "I've heard that the third lad is already on the way to try to rescue the reed-girl. I'm going to teach him a thing or two. I've hidden the ring in the Iron Hill."

In the morning the witch woke up the lad and asked: "Did you hear anything, Ivanko?"

"No, granny, I was sleeping like a log."

The boy was about to set off.

"I'll go with you," said the third cat. "We'll dupe the old hag. You're going to get hold of a cat and tie it to the pillar instead of me. The witch is old and weak-sighted, so she won't notice for some time."

Ivanko did everything as he was told.

They had walked they knew not how long when they found themselves in a vast field. Suddenly something hooted in the air and the cat said:

"The witch is already after us. Looks as if she has discovered the dummy. But I'll outwit her..."

The cat dug out the hole and said:

"Hide yourself here!"

Ivanko got into the hole and hid there together with the cat.

The Reed-Girl

The witch flew over them and disappeared in the distance.

Ivanko and the cat got out of the hole and went on. They walked for a day, for two days, and on the third day they came to a cave. The cat said:

"Here lives a sorcerer who bears a grudge against the old witch. You go in to talk to him and I'll hunt some mice around here."

The sorcerer was very ancient and as frail as flies in the fall. He lay there hardly breathing at all. He caught sight of Ivanko and said:

"It's nice of you to come here, lad. Bring me some water, please, for I can't stand up any more."

Ivanko fetched him some water, cooked a dinner and fed the old man. Grateful, the sorcerer told him his story:

"When I was young all witches deeply respected me. But when I became old the wretched creatures burned my book and abandoned me in this cave. Now that I have one foot in the grave, I'll share with you, lad, the biggest secret of all. You want to find the Iron Hill, don't you? Then give proper heed to what I shall say. Near the cave, at its southern side, I buried the magic shoes. Dig them out and they'll be yours. When you come to the sea throw them into the water and they'll turn into a boat that will take you to the Iron Hill. There is also a lake there from which no one has ever drunk..."

The sorcerer did not say another word. He closed his eyes and took his last breath.

Ivanko buried the sorcerer the way good people do. Then he dug out the magic shoes and set off, accompanied by the cat. They had been traveling for some time or so and eventually came to the shore of the blue sea the sorcerer had told about.

Ivanko threw the shoes into the water and in a flash a boat surfaced from under the water. They got on board and their voyage started. A day later they reached an island. When they went ashore the boat again turned into a pair of shoes.

The island was covered with very dense forest. Enormous trees rose high into the sky.

The cat climbed the tallest tree and scouted the area. He shouted:

"Ivanko, the Iron Hill is not far off!"

They ran in the direction suggested by the cat. At the foot of the mountain they plunged into the thickets looking for an entrance into the mountain. They kept silent and the mountain was quiet too.

Suddenly the mountain screeched and disclosed an opening. Twelve girls, baskets in their hands, emerged from the passage.

"Good day, girls," Ivanko greeted them. "Where are you going?"

"To gather berries. Who are you anyway?"

"I've come to pay you a visit."

"We can't recieve guests, it's simply not allowed. If our master, the giant, sees you, this visit will be your last one."

"Who are you then?"

"We are the prisoners of the giant."

"Isn't he afraid of letting you gather berries on your own?"

"No, he is not afraid, for it's impossible to flee from this island. There exists only one boat this sea wouldn't turn over."

The Reed-Girl

87

The Reed-Girl

"Where can it be found?"

"It's owned by a sorcerer who is about to settle his accounts with this life somewhere in a cave. Nothing can catch up with this boat."

Ivanko helped the girls to gather berries and he kept telling them how nice it was to live among people where there are no such thickets.

Then he asked:

"Do you happen to know where the giant hides his gold ring?"

"In the golden casket. And he keeps the key to this casket in his left ear. But you'll play with your live should you try to get hold of the key, for the giant will wake up and kill you right away. He is stronger than the mountain!"

"What should I do to get hold of the ring?"

"First you must take the key out of the giant's left ear and then set fire to his book of life that's lying on the table."

The girls gathered their baskets full of berries. When they came back to the mountain the passage opened and the lad, having mingled with the girls, went inside with them.

The giant was sleeping in an enormous hall, snoring so loudly that the mountain was shaking.

Ivanko quietly approached the ogre and took the key out of his left ear. He then took a flint, struck fire and blew on the kindling wood until it blazed. Then he set fire to the giant's book of life on the table.

The smoke, as black as pitch, rose up in the hall... The giant writhed in convulsions and then started to fade out: his feet vanished only to be followed by his body, hands, neck... A small part of the book somehow remained unscorched; it fell down on the earthern floor and the fire died out. The giant's eyes then rose up and went wandering around the hall. Ivanko stepped out from a dark corner, came to the golden casket, opened it and took out the ring. The giant's eyes were floating behind him but the lad was not at all scared. He opened the gate and shouted:

"Hey, girls! Will you bring me a jar to fill with the water from the lake from which no one has drunk yet?"

"Here you are," said the girls.

The cat led him to the lake. They filled the jar and the cat said:

"We must flee while the witch is still unaware of her son's death. She can do a lot of harm."

Currently they found themselves in front of a dreadful iron gate.

The Reed-Girl

"Ivanko, knock your gold key on it three times," said one of the girls.

The lad did so and the gate opened. Ivanko, the cat and the girls ran to the sea shore followed by the giant's eyes.

Ivanko threw the magic shoes into a wave and the boat surfaced from beneath it. They got aboard and sailed off. Ivanko turned round. On the shore the giant's eyes shone with tears as big and round as apples, which kept falling into the sea.

When they reached the opposite shore the girls ran out into a green field. Meanwhile the lad hid the magic shoes in his bossom and said:

"Now, my beautiful flowers, you'd best go home, for me and the cat must go our own way."

The girls thanked Ivanko and they parted.

The lad headed for the witch's hut. He poured the water from the jar onto the two stones and immediately

89

they turned into two nice lads who looked as if they had just woken up.

"We slept long, didn't we?" they said.

"Well, you would've slept till the end of the world had I not awoken you with the water from that jar. You may go home, lads. The witch, I reckon, has already lost all her power."

The lads left. Ivanko and the cat headed for the rushes on the bank of the river. The man took the ring and put it on top of the reed.

The reed swayed and in a flash turned into a girl, as beautiful as the first spring flower.

Ivanko said:

"I won't live a single day without you. Be my wife..."

The girl handed him the gold ring and they went to see her parents, who turned out to be decent Hutsuls, mourning for their beloved daughter.

People say that they got married and that the cat was always with them, spinning yarns and telling fairy tales.

Литературно-художественное издание

ЭХО ЗЕЛЕНЫХ ГОР

Украинские народные сказки

Перевод с украинского
С. А. Владова и М. Ф. Скрипник

Художник *Н. С. Пономаренко*

Киев, издательство художественной
литературы «Днипро»

На английском языке

Редактор *В. О. Баришев*
Художній редактор *О. Д. Назаренко*
Технічні редактори *Б. С. Грінберг,
Т. М. Мацапура*
Коректор *А. К. Вінярська*

ИБ № 4275

Здано до складання 28.09.87. Підписано до друку
16.05.88. Формат $70 \times 90^1/_{12}$. Папір офсетний.
Гарнітура таймс. Друк офсетний. Умовн. друк. арк.
8,97. Умовн. фарбовідб. 37,83.
Обл.-вид. арк. 5,663. Тираж 25 000 пр. Зам. 7—363.
Ціна 1 крб. 20 к.

Видавництво художньої літератури «Дніпро».
252601, Київ-МСП, вул. Володимирська, 42.

З текстових діапозитивів Головного
підприємства республіканського виробничого
об'єднання «Поліграфкнига»
на Київській книжковій фабриці «Жовтень».
252053, Київ, вул. Артема, 25.

*Ukrainian children's tales
in English translation with
many colourful illustrations
are regularly brought out
by Dnipro Publishers.*

*Place your orders at
bookstores in your country
which sell or distribute
Soviet books and periodicals.*

*For more information
write to:*

*DNIPRO PUBLISHERS
42 VOLODIMIRSKA ST.
KIEV, UKRAINIAN SSR
USSR*